350

Continued

Wesleyan Poetry

Piotr Sommer

Continued

Wesleyan University Press ■ Middletown, Connecticut

Published by Wesleyan University Press,
Middletown, CT 06459
www.wesleyan.edu/wespress
© 2005 by Piotr Sommer

Printed in the United States of America

Library of Congress
Cataloging-in-Publication Data
Sommer, Piotr, 1948–
    [Poems. English. Selections]
    Continued / Piotr Sommer.
        p. cm. — (Wesleyan poetry)
    ISBN 0-8195-6767-1 (cloth : alk. paper)
    —ISBN 0-8195-6768-x (pbk. : alk. paper)
    1. Sommer, Piotr, 1948 – Translations
    into English. I. Title. II. Series
    PG7178.O58A2 2005
    891.8'517 – dc22   2004061205

The publisher gratefully acknowledges the
cooperation of Bloodaxe Books, publishers
of the U.K. edition of this book.

Translated by

Halina Janod

&

Ed Adams

Jarosław Anders

John Ashbery

Edward Carey

Chad Chmielowicz

Douglas Dunn

D. J. Enright

Michael Kasper

W. Martin

Charles Mignon

Tadeusz Pióro

Mark Slobin

Elżbieta Volkmer

Contents

From elsewhere

From A Subsequent World / *Kolejny Świat* (1983)

From elsewhere

From What We're Remembered By / *Pamiątki po nas* (1980)

From elsewhere

From the American (1989)

Acknowledgments

Most of these poems were first published in the Polish collections listed in the table of contents. "Prospects in Prose," "Communication Department," "Sometimes, Yes," and "Great, Now What" first appeared in *Nowe stosunki wyrazów* (New relations of words, 1997). "Little Graves," "Confirmation," and "Other Half" appeared in *Kresy* 4 (1999) and *Res Publica Nowa* 12 (2002). The poems listed under the headings "From elsewhere" are arranged chronologically.

Sections of this book were published as *Things to Translate and Other Poems* (Bloodaxe Books, 1991). Grateful acknowledgments are also due to the editors of *Agni, Aufbau, Chicago Review, The Honest Ulsterman, The New Yorker, Orient Express, Poetry, Poetry Review, The Threepenny Review,* and *The Times Literary Supplement* in which other poems have since appeared.

Some of the translators — John Ashbery, Edward Carey, Douglas Dunn, D. J. Enright, Michael Kasper, W. Martin, and Mark Slobin — looked through other parts of the manuscript as well, and their suggestions substantially improved it. For other friendly comments, special thanks to Tamara Duvall, August Kleinzahler, Madeline Levine, Nancy Pick, Christopher Reid, Fiona Sampson, Henry Shukman, Greta Slobin, Łukasz Sommer, and Stephanie Steiker.

Foreword

Piotr Sommer's poetic excavations of the quotidian will, I hope, be a cause for real excitement among American readers unfamiliar with his work. The poems themselves are quite approachable and need little by way of explanation. But allow me to share a few thoughts about the work and the poet that may be helpful.

Sommer's everyday world is Poland, chiefly Warsaw and its suburbs, from the mid- to late twentieth century and into the first few years of our new century. It is a world saturated in history, almost all of it brutal and tragic, or, at the very least, difficult. But this is not Sommer's principal subject. Sommer the poet only happens to be Polish; the Polish situation — historical, political — though it colors the work and not infrequently intrudes upon it, is not what this poetry is really about. This is not a poetry that aspires to articulate the historical conscience of a people, nor would it presume to, which for some American readers might make it seem curiously un-Polish. The American reader will know soon enough he is in Poland and not Arcady or Cincinnati. Many of the poems are site-specific and filled with Polish names of people and places and things. Also, the feel of the poetry will, I think, identify it as Eastern European. It is not allegorical, symbolist, or parabolic, per se, but the work bears the inflections of those kinds of poetic treatment of subject matter to which the reader of translations from the Eastern European will be familiar.

Sommer's main subject is the "quandary-ness" of "ordinary life": an old dog, the color and texture of a lemon, an elevator in a dilapidated apartment building, the crash of toiletries on a bathroom floor. The art of the poetry — and its art is considerable, singular and memorable — is in the way it matter-of-factly transforms ordinary incident, character, landscape, object, and the assorted interactions thereof, into tiny metaphysical and epistemological essays: investigations into the subjects of language, imagination, impermanence, memory, identity. It is a poetry that engages large subjects through its attentiveness to seemingly small or minor events.

Sommer is not only a poet of importance but a significant translator of American and British poetry into Polish. He has produced Polish editions of Frank O'Hara and Charles Reznikoff, and Sommer's own poetry has been strongly influenced by the work of both Americans with its mix of off-handedness, the depoeticized treatment of subject matter, the focus on the domestic, the strangeness and significance of the minor and ephemeral, the manner in which the voice is handled. All of these characteristics he would have found in the work of the so-called New York Poets and Objectivists that he has translated. Still, I don't think the reader will be directly reminded of O'Hara, Reznikoff, or any other American poet in particular, including Robert Lowell, whom Sommer has also translated. Sommer's influences, which are broad, appear to have been thoroughly digested. If his poetry has any identifiable antecedents, I would suggest that they are French, as befits the son of a partly French mother. Follain and Ponge come to mind.

As a translator of poetry from English who has also spent a great deal of time in America and Britain imaginatively and in fact, many of Sommer's poems have a rather liminal feel about them, of poetic incident and impulse caught up in the act of being translated into language, a language, but one that refracts and interacts with a secondary or alternative language. Meaning is unstable. There is a quality of otherness in the poetry, or the suggestion of otherness. Boundaries are continually being crossed. There are sallies and retreats. What at first reading may seem straightforward is, in fact, rather craftily and carefully assembled and held taut in a web of contingencies. Sommer is very much the poet as double agent, working both sides of the border and traveling incognito.

The translator of poetry knows better than anyone else the difficulties and loss incurred by the passage of a poem from one language to another. In Polish, Sommer is an intensely musical poet. I know because I've heard him read aloud. His poems move in a complex array of measures. They make gorgeous noises with their textures of consonants and vowels. Sommer's poetry also makes very particular use of colloquial diction and constructions to achieve its effects in Polish. Many, perhaps most, of these effects do not make the passage into English, and much of the music of the originals has been sacrificed. But if we do not get the full glory of Sommer's poetry in English translation, we still get a great deal, which is testimony both to the poetry and the quality of the translations.

The chief notion I would suggest to the new reader of this poetry is how Sommer, often several times within a given poem, establishes tonalities and then modulates them into alternative tonalities in such a way that the quiddity of the piece becomes unpredictable and subject to transformation at any point, say from irony to pity and back again. Any given poem has multiple planes and surfaces, many of these not immediately evident until turned sideways, ever so slightly, by an unexpected word or syntactical effect that provokes entirely new possibilities and resonances of meaning.

Sommer's poetry is distinguished, on the one hand, by an uncommon breadth of sympathies and its humanness, as full of heart as it is of intellect. It is also a poetry of trap doors, false bottoms, and numerous levers, some real, some faux, that the poet invites readers to pull at their own discretion. With regard to this last, allow me to caution the reader: should you pull the wrong (or right) lever, you may find any number of your habits of mind set on their head, likewise your expectations of how language and meaning interrelate. So be alert. Exercise caution. Go slowly. And enjoy the ride.

August Kleinzahler
San Francisco
August 2004

Shepherd's Song

Morning on Earth

Morning on earth, light snow, and just when
it was so warm, practically spring.
But the thermometer in the kitchen window
says seven degrees,
and pretty sunny.
                    Here's
the electric company guy I like,
and no sign of the gas guy
I can't stand.
And all of a sudden two Misters M. —
one I've fallen for, the other
a bit of a hotshot —
coming back, both nine years old,
just passing the jasmine bush,
a huge bouquet of sticks.
                         Behind the door
the dog's excited, nothing's
at odds with anything.

Yesterday

Autumn on small plots ringing the houses —
except for the few jasmines still
clothed and sparrows
hopping from one lilac bush

to another — does it really make for such a naked
moral? such a come-down? a message
of leaves behind the rusted fence
protecting us so nicely

from the eyes of the passer-by and of the neighbor
who long long ago worked in the passport office,
and from the headlights chasing leaves

like the wind, only faster faster and
maybe it's because of this momentum
you quicken your pace

Visibility

We ride the ridge, by track and tunnel,
then after a while
descend, but first
there are brooks and bridgelets, because

how can they call them bridges,
yesterday Smithy, before that Hebden,
and now Sowerby and purple foxgloves
on the embankment. And still

I haven't figured out who
I'm saying this to, or even who
would care that through the leaves

you can see Halifax
and someone's life, June being so transparent,
though yesterday it rained and clouds came out.

Municipal Services

On the second anniversary, oddly, there wasn't time,
just snow, which amounts to the same thing.
I was moving in water up to my mouth,
though the streets were cleared faster
than the snow could fall.

I was waving my arms about, I was gathering air,
I went back to my rented home
but I couldn't concentrate on sleeping.
I got the order confused, and the new one
seemed to me more beautiful.

If you have any plans of coming back,
at most I'll miss my stop, I'll overshoot
a continent, I'll open my mouth and won't reply
to the question I have no answer for.

Continued

Nothing will be the same as it was,
even enjoying the same things
won't be the same. Our sorrows
will differ one from the other and we
will differ one from the other in our worries.

And nothing will be the same as it was,
nothing at all. Simple thoughts will sound
different, newer, since they'll be more simply, more newly
spoken. The heart will know how to open up and love
won't be love anymore. Everything will change.

Nothing will be the same as it was
and that too will be new somehow, since after all,
before, things could be similar: morning,
the rest of the day, evening and night, but not now.

i.m. Milton Hindus
1916–1998

And later just to look into their papers,
half-read in their lifetime, letters —
if there were a place to keep them
and they hadn't been chewed up by mice in the attic

or soiled by the marten
which no one ever saw but everyone
suspected of subletting — or even
to enter them by hand into hard memory

since that might be the way to treat them
to a new time, another round —
not that we have more of it now,
but, older for a moment, we can almost see them

the way they wanted to be seen,
"With a New Preface by the Author," in which
with us in mind, who else,
they still managed to correct this or that.

Short Version

I couldn't be with you when you died.
Sorry, I was toiling day and night
on the title of a poem I didn't have time to show you.
You really would have liked it.

Even if the poem itself
wasn't the strongest, I was counting on the title
to prop it up from above,
to set it right even, and to sanction it

as sometimes happens, I don't know
if the nurse ever had time
to give you the news

because when I called it was
already late, though finally
she took the whole message.

Tomorrow

Whoever lives on will tell us how it was; whoever survives the rest will tell it more precisely.

Shepherd's Song

Read these few sentences as if I were
some stranger, some other
language, which I may still be
(though I speak with your words, make use
of your words);
which I was, speaking
your language,
standing behind you and listening
wordlessly,
singing
in your tongue
my tune.
Read as if you were to listen,
not to understand.

Sometimes, Yes

After reading certain young authors
I too would like to be an author
and turn out works.
Right now I'm thinking of J.G. —
his happy rhymes, cinematic sentences and
the heroes in his poems, the real ones
and those made up. Because of course
poems have their heroes as well,
some not even all that
likeable. Of the real ones
for instance, I recall
Ezra Pound, whose name
appears in one of the titles,
or that Mid-November Snow
which, before it melted, the author thinks
had blanketed all the evil.
Of the unreal ones Kirillov, a suicide
and yet a builder, or that
professor, what's his name,
a scholar of seventy now.

And I, what would I write poems about?
I'd have to think,
because in fact I'm fed up with them.
I ask my wife but she just repeats
"What about?" as if she weren't there.
And a moment later adds: "But if
I tell you what about, you'll say
we both wrote it, all right?"
I must — she says — remind her
about it in the future, since a person
may sometimes really get hold of an idea,
but most of the time it flies off.

Lyric Factor and Other Poems

Indiscretions

Where are we? In ironies
that no one will grasp, short-lived
and unmarked, in trivial points
which reduce metaphysics to absurd
detail, in Tuesday that falls on
day two of May, in mnemonics of days.
You can give an example or take it
on faith, cat's paw at the throat.

And one also likes certain words and those — pardon me —
syntaxes that pretend that something links them together.
Between these intermeanings the whole man is contained,
squeezing in where he sees a little space.

Candle

Friends from long ago, loved unchangingly,
with whom you could talk, talk until exhausted —
well, they must have forgotten some mutual concern,
or potentially mutual.
And new ones? New ones keep quiet,
as if they wanted to say nothing
more than necessary.

Amnesia

I forget about the other world.
I wake up with my mouth closed,
I wash the fruit with my mouth closed,
smiling, I bring the fruit into the room.
I don't know why I remember cod-liver oil,
whole years of misery, the cellar bolt on the floor,
the self-sufficient voice of the grandmother.
Still, this is not the other world.
And again I sit at the table with my mouth closed
and you bring me delicious bursting plums
and I repeat after someone I also forget:
there is no other world.

Station Lights

Station lights connect with those above,
the days of the week connect,
the wind with the breath —
there's nothing that doesn't.

The broken heating plant in Żerań
and my child, and the woman
I picked out years ago because of
her white knee-socks with blue stripes.

Interesting how the world
connects tomorrow and the day after that.
If that's not it,
maybe you'll tell me what is.

Landscape with Branch

We're bound to one another
by unknown threads, a stitch
of corpuscles that sew up the globe.
One day the globe
drops from us,
shrinks and dries
like a blackthorn plum —

something was really ours,
but we no longer belong to things.

Transparencies

The afternoon sun
round the corner of the town,
and every inch of skin
and every thought
is clearly exposed,
and nothing can be hidden
as everything comes to the surface:
unanswered letters,
ingratitude,
short memory.

Innocence

When we first met, we were really so young.
I saw nothing wrong in writing poems about myself.
Didn't I know that I too would be ashamed of something?
Didn't I know who you were?

Shame and laughter lock my mouth in turn.
I'm ashamed to think of it; I'm amused to be ashamed.

Believe me

You're not going to find a better place
for these cosmetics, even if eventually
we wind up with some sort of bathroom cabinet and
you stop knocking them over with your towel —
there'll still be a thousand reasons to complain
and a thousand pieces of glass on the floor
and a thousand new worries,
and we'll still have to get up early.

Home and Night

A day of sleeping and writing letters, of plasticine and games.
In place of dots the dominoes have animals,
Crude shapes of animals on shoddy plastic.
A world without abstraction.
It cost sixty-eight złotys.
Everything's dearer and more primitive.
Could life by day be less complicated?
Yes. But the dominoes are blue,
blue plastic with gold animals,
and life is black and white.

Guesswork

She's covering her eyes, but doesn't she even hear
what I'm thinking and why? That
no one knows. Even this thought-and-written sentence
has two true endings, like a wire,
a length of wire, a trans-
continental transnational cable,
witness to daily betrayals and lies
by politicians and priests, like a broken string.
And who is it now who covers her eyes and hears nothing,
confusing light with the music of certain spheres?

Days of the Week

Tomorrow is Thursday.
If the world meets its obligations,
the following day will be Friday.
If it doesn't, it could even be Sunday,
and no one will ever guess
where our life got mislaid.

Travel Permit, Round Trip

A small calf on a cart, on cobblestones, happily whisking his tail, a Polish stork, lost in thought, a peasant woman wearing, as you'd expect, a kerchief on her head. A basket in her hand. The landscape rolls along at the same, steady pace, without stopping, and then illogically veils itself with hills.

I switch seats with a child who would rather watch the world unroll.

The tape is winding up somewhere on the other side and the reel must already be bulging. It contains so much, all that and this too, the perpetual policemen, by trade and calling, stalking furiously, and these light-hearted village names: Pszczółki, Szymankowo.

My face may be still, but in my heart I'm bursting with laughter. We're allowed to travel by train again. This delicate pressure on my arm is only your sleep.

Leaves and Comes Back

There's yet another life, lived in brief, also unacknowledged. A woman with a dog, a black poodle, outside the window of Telimena on Krakowskie Przedmieście, passes by and vanishes, as if she had no meaning. Life half-imagined, half-observed.

Vanishes, while from the opposite direction another elderly woman appears, with a plastic bag, she must be going shopping. But in the shop next door there's still no bread, and still no papers at the kiosk. Yet everything's right today: the morning, the imagination, the waitress bringing coffee, sight.

A little hedge in the square facing Dziekanka suddenly takes on a different color. Green, but more intense, and even the steel-gray uniform of a militiaman – who, there's no knowing why, makes for the Mickiewicz monument – is more familiar, though not quite mine. Perhaps he wants to take a closer look.

I don't know whether the world this autumn truly has more dignity or whether it just seems so. Besides, now memory wants to mix in: the gas in '68, the old dog Frendek licking up his own blood, other months, other seasons.

I guess you can really put your life in order, can live with less. But the heart, the heart doesn't give up easily, and goes on knocking, and the eye, in its usual way, alters backgrounds and planes. The tongue builds sentences, the body trembles slightly.

Medicine

Again I've seen a genuine lemon.
Ania brought it back for me from France.
She thought: return, or else stay on?
And what good reason holds her here —
a few faces, and words, and this anxiety?
The lemon was yellow and looked genuine.
No need to display it in the window
so it could come to itself, like our pale tomatoes,
or as we come to ourselves,
ripening and yellowing for years.
No, it was fully itself already
when she brought it, not so much yellow
as gold, and slightly gnarled.
So I accepted it gratefully.

I'd like to put on the thick skin of the world,
I'd like to be tart but on the whole tasty —
a child swallows me unwillingly,
and I'm good for his cold.

According to Brecht

I suspect certain poets
have recently stopped submitting their poems to journals.
They must be thinking: we'll wait
until all this calms down
and they (journals
and other poets) get over this infantile disease
of civic-mindedness
or whatever you call it.
As they will.
Readers will get fed up with it,
editors will get bored too, and finally
they'll turn to us.
And we'll open our drawers
and take out our Timeless Values
which, precisely because they're timeless,
can now
wait calmly.

A Certain Tree in Powązki Cemetery

All memory we owe to objects
which adopt us for life and
tame us with touch, smell
and rustle. That's why it's so hard
for them to part with us: they guide us
till the end, through the world,
till the end they use us, surprised
by our coolness and the ingratitude
of that famous spinner Mnemosyne.

Fragile

I was going to sleep
not remembering a thing,
just scrunching up on the side of the bed,
knowing I should leave room.

I began the year washing dishes.
The water was warm, it was nobody's,
I didn't have to hurry.
Before my eyes

stood all the verbs,
to be, to write, to love,
all tangled up for years.
I didn't have to remember anything

although the mouth monotonously
repeated the word
memory, memory, memory
as if beyond it

nothing meant anything.
And without willing it,
already on the edge of sleep,
I saw your face again

as it was a few hours back,
last year,
tired, but still beautiful,
dark blue like a swallow,

almost raven black,
and the face of a seven-year-old boy,

composed and delicate,
just about to smile;

your black hair
brightened against the child's light mop,
the mouth kept whispering memory, memory.
Drops of sleep ran down the pane of the eye.

Don't Sleep, Take Notes

At four in the morning
the milkwoman was knocking
in plain clothes, threatening
she wouldn't leave us anything,
at most remove the empties,
if I didn't produce the receipt.

It was somewhere in my jacket,
but in any case I knew
what the outcome would be:
she'd take away yesterday's curds,
she'd take the cheese and eggs,
she'd take our flat away,
she'd take away the child.

If I don't produce the receipt,
if I don't find the receipt,
the milkwoman will cut our throats.

Third State

Out of nowhere I remembered dawn
and it was almost like in childhood—
the soul tore itself from the body,
it saw right through it from above,

unattached now for good
to its evacuated comical form
which can't even get off the ground.
It saw the body, but didn't know

how clumsy it really was,
wingless for eternity.
I myself must have been off to the side
because I saw them both

through the morning half-light, strangely clear,
as if it wasn't winter,
or fog, or buildings getting in the way.
And I was between them both

like a third, an odd shoe,
I'm not quite sure where,
off to the side, but near,
hidden now in a nook of the soul

floating lightly through space, now
in its corporal shell, looking up
with sincere regret. Then in the air
a mantel of snow was flapped

threadbare, riddled with holes,
and people's faces down below were also white.
I rippled down, conjoined, and soaked
into the city.

Liberation, in Language

These heart-stirring errors of craft—
uncertainty how a nation
should respond to violence,
made up for by an urgent
sense of mission
(words big as beans
that are hard to swallow)
and that almost obsessive
lack of detail—

yes, one can speak this way
from the stage: this language
is not beautiful but all
abruptly draw out their hands
and clap, and so, perforce,
it must be correct.

Landscape with Wind

Metal oxides, black lung
(take shallow breaths)
the dust of the world
pierced by headlights

eye-to-eye housing estates
(take no notice)
and at daybreak
four chipboards' worth of sleep

full of stinging fog
and men in masks
squares and streets
(don't cry, don't get upset)

Worldliness

Hearing the lift coming up,
voices on the stairs, a brief argument,
the old dog is drawn away from her blanket
and the contemplation of another world,
and reluctantly strolls over to the door
to express her opinion. She favors
the worldly life, but without conviction.

Neolith

By chance, while talking with Paweł,
the word "neolith" comes up, possibly because of
the beautiful picture book *Before Man Appeared*,
which we gave our son for his birthday.

I talk and at the same time look
at my son modeling little plasticine animals,
and my eye suddenly falls
on Paweł's ear, delicate, its design
different from mine, and big a brim-cap.
Paweł's ear, which like the rest of Paweł,
his thin hair, his nose and eyes,
his careful mind as well as
his biggish feet,
will turn thirty in four days.

Thirty in four days.
Mid-April, the height of spring.
Half life or just a third?
Haste or impatience?
Involuntarily, I look more and more intently
at Paweł's softly blossoming ear,
autumnal rather, the color
of unscythed corn, a color, who
knows why, there's still too little of,
but more to come.

Talkativeness

But the citizen should be honest
and tell everything —
after all, the phones have been reconnected
so that he could
communicate with friends
or whoever he wants,
and it would be highly immoral
and, frankly speaking, quite unfair
to ring a friend
and not tell him everything
hinting
in addition
that one knows much more

Grammar

What was, one should speak of in the past tense,
what isn't, in some other tongue.

Ah, Continuity

This song might be right, pal,
but don't sing it to me again:
its refrain pulses even in the roots
of pines, its echo hanging over the tips
of grasses, its lyric known well to the world's memory—
that black horse of hope, which says
nothing.

Lighter, Darker

I ask questions
when I should finally be giving some answers.
I don't know who I'm directing them to
or if I'm directing them to anyone at all.
I hear how the child calls out in sleep —
for seven years, each year, these dreams
are more and more intense,
the calling becomes a shout,
the shouting more assertive.
I think too slowly, I feel faster.
A mania for precision, after a few years' experience,
stops being tiring, boring, and obtrusive.
Shreds of plot come by themselves
and arrange themselves in the right order,
precisely — not at all the way it was.
The device for asking questions,
privilege of immaturity,
sputters, stops, and falls asleep.
I wake up staring at the family screen
where one dream-frame has frozen.

What was unacceptable
becoming acceptable.

Proofs

Don't worry about commas, all these
punctuation marks, colons, semi-colons
and dashes which you so scrupulously
specify will be, thanks to a proof-
reader's inattentiveness, left out; the rhythm
of your sentence, your thinking, your language
will prove less important than
you expected, or maybe than you wanted.
That was nothing but wishful thinking —
you won't be read to the music of speech
but to the hubbub of things.

Apolitical Poem

Nature's motor ticked, chirped and bubbled,
hummed and rumbled, almost swelled,
although the river was shallow,
small, in fact a brook,

the late-day sun was warm,
no rain fell, and crickets
changed shifts smoothly, technically perfect —
you couldn't hear the gaps, it was like

some absolutely packed silence:
the mechanism ran on steadily
and didn't choke at all
on itself or on the surfeit of voices as if

still covered by warranty
issued by god knows who,
without stamps, without paperwork —
with a handshake, or even with the wind —

and yet in the machinery
everything played on, rolling
not quite so evenly, now nearer,
now further off, from all sides,

moderately or forcefully, as it
pleased, like an orchestra
whose particular components, primary
parts — the instruments

and maybe the audience too,
the blades of grass

my eyes surveyed, nettles and ferns —
didn't move, just

stood there
as if they were either dead or
still had time, or
patience.

Ode to the Carnival

But of course we'll travel together one day,
maybe not right now and not precisely where we had in mind,
maybe somewhere else, it's hard to say where,
but almost certainly this trip will work out
not just for us obviously,
all our loved ones will come along, kids,
friends, I mean people you can even
have a quarrel with, just a few, a fair chunk
of the world, which for the hell of it got
that legendary passport, not yet, of course,
but any day now, and then they'll take this ride,
flight, cruise, our parents even
could join us, why not, if any of them
want to, if they've still got a bit of get-up-and-go,
and fancy seeing the world, too, after all these years,
so don't worry about a thing, because
definitely one day we'll make that jaunt
abroad, it'll be almost like a real
foray across the border which didn't
work out for us in seventy-something-
or-other or in eighty and eighty
-one, two, three and
four and now in eighty-five
which is also drawing to an end, and once again
we won't have to talk so much
because words will be harmless as confetti

Don't Worry, It Won't Get Lost

How could I fail to understand how you feel
even if personally I never lost
a PKO bankbook with my life
savings in it. Yet meanwhile
the radio's on, and glancing through the window
I see, on the empty street,
a forty-year-old with whom yesterday
I sat for a few years
on the same school bench, the knocking of the mangle
is heard under the floor, and even
on the balcony clothesline
a brown-and-white butterfly has landed. I have
some shopping to do, a train to catch,
there's only a few dozen złotys
in my pocket, but the keys
jingle when I brush them,
the street is getting peopled, pockets
are filling up.

Receding Planets of the Rowan Tree

There's always something more important — little bottles
half-filled with Cardiamid-and-Caffeine,
still alive, even when empty
they're alive, since they stand by
the basket of bread and the Homemade Gingerbread Mix
and the still untouched jar of Herb Honey. The untidied
apartment is alive —
not something, it's life that is more important.

The enlarged liver
doesn't have to mean the worst.
It could have tired itself with hormones,
brown bread and a bit of pork.

The table drawer
full of odds and ends
would no longer be alive
if it were put straight.
If books were ordered in the closet,
the photos in the album, the rest of the dirty clothes
washed, the room repainted —
they too would no longer live.

It's necessary to eat, take medicines, put
the bowl by the bed, get out of bed,
make tea and
call the doctor
who won't wipe his shoes
but mechanically writing out
the prescription, will say: you have
a nice picture there, madam.

As a matter of fact
very nice,
especially in the afternoon,
when it catches the sun.

(November 1985)

Out of Town

Years later, the water still drips —
there's no one to tighten the valve.
It courses through old pipes
down to the septic tank.

Next morning in the cellar
I start the motor with a stick.
It shakes and rumbles, and chirps —
the switch is broken is all.

At night the water arrives
illegally, undergroundly,
to the very grave where
last spring parsley sprouted,

and at the foot, beside it,
feral sorrel darkens
tastily and tartly
like clandestine sex.

The motor lifts the spirits
and returns the night's deductions.
It's morning, I hum softly —
a stranger will replace me.

In the cellar a stream of light
rinses the window grate,
it pulses, strikes the meter —
I catch my rhythm on the stairs.

And for memory's sake I hum —
as I pass the septic tank —
a fluid, underground song
about sorrel and a stranger.

Prospects in Prose

I dreamt I was smoking a cigarette
and cold Elżbieta Z. from Otwock
was peering over her glasses in a huge
department store full of merchandise
stocked like in the West, where
she was a shop girl, and chocolate,
if I read the price correctly, cost
exactly 1,087 złotys.
Elżbieta
had white, slightly gelatinous
flesh, heavyish but
sweet in its own way, just like
Maciek told me.
Crates
smelled of late-harvest grapes, and I
pinched one between one puff
of smoke and the next so nobody
would collar me, beats me why frankly, since
I had the cash, that much I remember,
which seemed western, too.
I must've
swiped something else, for I left on the sly
pretending to walk straight, like I wasn't
scared of anything, and yet afraid
to talk to her.
My face
was still a boy's, I knew it
by how I walked, Mother wasn't
sick yet, my son, though little,
was growing moderately well, and everywhere
they even had sugar galore.

A Small Treatise on Non-Contradiction

Son goes out of the apartment block to get some air
since the fall is still pretty, and why waste the weather.
He goes to the pond to study bugs, returns
and checks everything in books.

From the kitchen window I watch the boys kick a ball.
The door opens, and while the door's open
you can hear that the elevator works today,
clicks shut and moves on, to be useful.

A Maple Leaf

A maple leaf with the sun shining through it
at the end of summer is beautiful, but
not excessively so, and even an ordinary
electric train passing by
nearly three hundred yards away
makes music, light and unobtrusive,
and yet to be remembered, for its own sort of
usefulness perhaps, or even
instructiveness (the world somehow
doesn't quite say it knows everything,
has a good memory and, above all,
won't show it off)

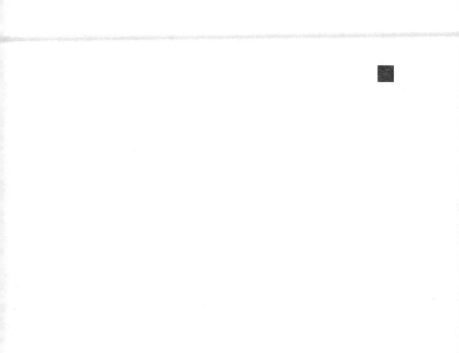

Little Graves

I come to see Maciek after several years,
and already they have a calm, healthy child,
who sleeps and doesn't want to show her eyes.
They call her Maryśka.
Maryśka has just turned thirteen days old, but then
she's three weeks, and now she shows
one eye, and peeks up, a little to the right.
Maciek says "Maryśka," "Marychna,"
as if he were getting used to it,
gently, paternally, and Agnieszka,
who has as many meat coupons as a miner,
and who's dripping with milk,
starts clucking her tongue at her.

The white of the other eye, the unfixed gaze, open mouth,
tongue sticking out, the whole concentrated face.
I look at the mystery of the navel, at the fleshy vulva,
which seems disproportionately large —
it will probably be Agnieszka who informs her about those things;
Maciek doesn't like the word "vulva," maybe
some bad experience. Milk
pours into her mouth. Walking downstairs,
we hear her choking, then she's all right.
We sit, we smoke — All Saints' Day in three weeks.

A week or two after my son was born
I kicked two of his mother's aunts down the stairs, well,
almost, no violence involved. One of them
bent over him without taking off her coat, the other
was ready, it seems, to give him a bath,
or maybe just some advice.
Everybody could see I was being rational, but our rations

started to shrink soon after, to shrink before us,
and in the back, whatever that might mean.
What's more, the one with the bath
used to sell meat in a meat store
long before they had coupons ho ho.
Well, we used to be impulsive,
and could really hold a grudge, solemn
and brief, like a resolution to improve,
until the judgment — or what do you call it — the fatal day!

Besides, we do need to forgive.
How else could we survive, all swollen with pain
that won't condense or liquefy, but is always there —
though one doesn't have to say right away
that one has forgiven. With Maciek,
I either told him
or somehow let him know,
but if I'd done to him what he did to me,
I wouldn't believe such declarations, either.
My thing is talking,
but in fact I like to listen, that is, to ask things.
And give names —
when the time is right.

And me, where will I lie in the end?
In Powązki, in France, in Łódź, in Otwock?
Or perhaps, God only knows,
since God knows everything, in some
completely foreign country? Impossible.
Lately I don't even want to
talk about it, because we always fight,
that is, if silence, or
singing out of spite (tra la),
can be called fighting.
Besides, is it worth it —

and what if they ship me out to rest
in Wałbrzych?

Maciek wakes me up at half past ten.
I go back to bed for ten more minutes, and get up—
at twelve.
Tea!
Bread (with cheese).
A sprint to the florist—a basket of violets
for the doctor who operated on my mother.

We leave the hospital, arms locked,
slowly, but—
I'm forgetting,
it wasn't such an easy surgery.
At home my mother lies down,
and I go out to make calls,
run errands,
have coffee,
I come back, and we have supper.
Because there's still no
curfew, no gas rations yet,
no passports needed to go from Otwock to Świder, because the air
is clean and it's evening, I go see Maciek.
Tomorrow Marysia will successfully complete her first half-year,
or: will begin, gloriously and without pain,
her second six months.
Maciek turns on the light,
I lean over the netting of her bed,
and Marysia smiles at me.

Of course, why should Maciek be wondering
where Agnieszka will lie?
Agnieszka looks good,
she's lost weight, has a new haircut with curls—

must have got it at Janek's,
and she's excitedly telling us
how Jacek bawled her out.
One thing is certain: in Otwock, where else.

Jacek, no doubt, will lie somewhere in Australia,
because there's a lot of sun there,
and plenty of room,
tra la,
unless he ends up
in some West Germany or other,
together with his son
and his wife, if
she stays with him.

A Subsequent World

The January Star

Yes, I remember the woman
I passed on December 31, 1976,
having said good-bye to Mother and my child,
heading for the station, near the optician's sign,
by the little hill where children were sledding.
Evening had already set in
and soon the world would be conveyed
into the night of the new year.
I'd seen her before in different parts of town,
and years ago my mother
had worked directly under her.
For a while I'd nodded hello.

Now she was walking toward me, not recognizing,
muffled up to her ears in a cheap fur coat,
tiny and old, slightly hunched
and, as always, spectacled.
And, I remember, walking by
I thought how long she'd worked
for the coat she had on now.
I must have been too detached
from that December, from children on sleds,
from the whole world, for it to make
any sense, without comparing her
to anyone else, anyone happier.
I saw her at the end of her life
and in passing; above the station, a January star kept swelling,
and on the train some other old woman
sat beside me.

Mikuś, Adam, Wieniek, and Me

And all this in front of the mirror
of my grandmother's old wardrobe.
Wieniek strums the bald head
of a wicker carpet-beater
whose oak shaft
becomes a neck.
Adam buries his lips
in the dark hole
of a big cardboard tube.
Mikuś and I wrestle
for the clarinet, a mountaineer's cane
whose origins I've forgotten —
even though we just agreed
that this time he
would bang the table!
But we were always
one too few,
and someone had to be
a multi-instrumentalist;
anyway, we all doubled parts,
sometimes from forgetfulness.
I don't remember, but it's likely
I really was worried about the neighbors.

The repertoire was extensive —
the whole gamut of standards.
Only later, when Mikuś
borrowed a real licorice stick,
we had to decide on something: he
handled the "Grandpa Polka" best, and I
picked up some skill
in Bechet's "Egyptian Fantasy" —

the age of specialization was on its way.

Easter

Let's go places
we've been before,
visit old friends,
learn who this
or that one is. They have
hands of gold and may live
a little differently today.

One sells dachshunds;
with the last litter he covered his roof.
Another fences stuff
or maybe just receives it
and moves it from place to place.
The third experiments
with his friend's words

to see if the friendship's
survived and if it has made sense.
In fact, the experiment proves
it hasn't.
And yet another one works
as a menial in Świerk:
at home, the wife, a three-year-old,

the wife's mother, the silent father-in-law.
So let's go to the old haunts,
we'll take the children for a walk,
and in the afternoon, eating a piece of cake,
we'll watch television together.
Let's go and see a friend to find out
who we are; he probably knows.

Celebrations

And there are always some old people coming from far away
for the holidays;
strangers, relatives
of your wife or of people you know.
You usually see them
for the last time and sometimes
for the first, almost like portraits
by old masters in a small
exhibition. They want to stay
sprightly and they smile
to you, to a few others,
as though they wished to fix
their photos in the air. Look,
the whites of their eyes jiggle.

Meanwhile the food's getting cold,
vodka in tumblers
is taking on the taste of glass, and they
talk on, pushing their homemade cake
toward you. The men
are drowsy, the children sleep.

But almost always
someone listens to the end —
a timid, well-bred
young man; old enough
to drink vodka
with the grown-ups, he's still
a bit uneasy
with women, he's still single
and now he nods politely at the words

of a charming old lady, whom he'll wind up
taking to the station
tomorrow
after breakfast.

Line

It's probably all about
this clean line — Japanese poets,
seventeenth, eighteenth century.
Probably in a small town
which you know well or at least
visited once or twice,
with pines and wooden houses,
a café, a church, a derelict Jewish graveyard.
Probably something still remains
in the portfolio of an amateur photographer
(who most likely goes to the capital once a week
to capture scenes), unless
he's already cropped
these black-and-white trees
and lilac bushes — perhaps not yet.
It's probably about
a drawing with children, a swing,
a queue outside the shop, with a dog even,
a mutt caught by the dog-catcher
taken away on a flat cart seventeen years ago;
with a candle stub when the light goes out
and when you have to go to bed by candlelight.
The drawing's to be clean:
underwear dries on a line,
a blue pajama top's just falling to the ground,
louder and louder someone's voice calls out "Jurek, Jurek";
next to the house, in the woods,
Jurek's sister collects brush.

A Visit

Someone was pounding on the eaves all night long.
It was my old friend Heniek Kowalski from Świętojańska Street.
His wonderful, tiny, bald father played at the Operetta.
Oh, they all played
until they went away.

And Kuba played cello and collected stamps.
Kuba met me in Warsaw just before he left.
I was doubly ashamed,
for myself and for everything else.

They all left as well —
our beautiful girls, a little older than us.
Left as well.
When I used to visit, he practiced violin.
Tonight, Heniek pounded the gutter;
it was a *tarka*, a washboard.

Once he announced "An Upbeat Song" and everybody laughed.
On banjo: Grzegorz Brudko, who hadn't met me.
When Heniek argued with his mother, the machine stopped
    sewing,
his father broke in, and Kuba some five years younger,
and the gray-haired aunt Estera Kowalska.

It was a real Tower of Babel, the raging tongues.
I waited for it all to end.
It must have been his mother, all night long
sewing Heniek's shirt with rain.
The old sewing machine wrenched the thread.
It was an intermittent knocking of the heart.

Small Cripplings

A child may be crippled only slightly —
some gloomy trace of brushing up against
a too-ghastly dream, probably
still in his mother's womb
or maybe somewhere else entirely,
I don't know where.

This three-and-a-half or maybe
four-year-old boy still
isn't aware of
his harelip.
Otherwise, he's pretty
and nicely dressed, and must
sometimes go with his young mama
to a café. But he still doesn't realize
he's not supposed to look at me
so normally, or exaggerate:
bug out his eyes, make faces,
chatter, puff out his cheeks,
like any other child.

Sooner or later it'll turn out
that in his mouth everything
sounds odd, and that the grins
don't fit his face,
though now his mother's words
mean only what they're meant to:
"Come to mommy,
stop bothering the man, you'll get a little cake."

And he'll go to her
and if you ask him if he liked it,
he'll probably say yes.

Hi, Helena

Helena asks, how's Jola's thesis.
So far no more than ten pages.
Helena nods. I guess she's thinking
about the burnt-out, frittered-away
promise of some young women
she knows who might still bear a child.
Does she have enough time for it?
Well yes, I say, as if my belly hurts.
Helena agrees that it's all about just getting going.

You can't get away from numbers. Not quite
ten pages of a belated master's thesis,
not quite six hours' sleep, a child
or two. In a few years
a next-of-kin dies and the young thirty-somethings
will open up the mortal flat
to live in it, like it or not
they'll move in, like it or not they'll forget
who left it to them.
Death wishes you all the very best.

But then what's the hurry, Helena adds.
Her husband got fired last year.
It's possible, even certain
that everything boils down to personally
certifying a few of the things that count. Many
won't even know
the story. I'm talking about all this
on the last day of August, a transparent night,
while well-wishing death keeps working
for another world, for us and ours.

Space

(after Wang Wei)

We live secluded under the smoke of steelworks.
The area to the east and south is Warsaw.
The sun is burning out and shining through the dust.
The river is invisible, our house was built by little ants.
It's freezing and almost dark, white figures return to their homes.
The buses can hardly move —
at home dogs have had a hard day.

Today, just as before, there are redundant people.
Yet each of them can do a lot and each can bear a lot.

Standards from the Seventies

And so one can talk not only about what one does,
but for example how to live, and what comes of it.
And what does one live?
One lives dead streets, rebuilt now for years,
the touch of your slim hand, the ungathered building blocks.
The days want to fill up in order to crack open.

Acquaintances listen with curiosity to a digression
about a good dentist who just does her work.
I look at the half-open mouth of a thirty-five-year-old man
sitting opposite, leafing through *A Puzzle Buff's Calendar 1979* —
he's either quite astonished or has a stuffy nose.

We get off first: a crossing, a green light,
we take the elevator up. A neighbor from the sixth floor
stomps out his cigarette butt and kicks it down the shaft.

Stasiek is probably right: the theme is not the point,
especially when it plays itself.
Real life doesn't.
Even a weak theme, done well,
will play itself —
and that's what you call real life!

I saw two old women talking in the middle of the sidewalk.

And I kept going.

I saw a bald man holding a small package wrapped in white paper and tied with plain string!

I looked back at him!

I saw a gas station with a row of vehicles — cars and trucks, and a man in gray overalls with a huge funnel in his hand, and the wind carried the smell of gas all the way to me on the other side —

I went right past it!

Yet another man, with a week's stubble, somewhere near forty, shouted "Antonio!" like an Italian, from across the street, but the guy he was calling was Polish too, like me and the "half percent of others," just ten years more worn out.

I kept going, the street smiled at me with open windows, sobbed to me, sang me a city song and I sang the refrain: sure, sure, we will rebuild.

Another World

I talk about children all the time.
Tenderness and madness,
quiet answers to questions and their cries in dreams.
There are more of them and they're bigger and bigger,
they memorize whole books and reproduce them
turning pages and drawing, drawing
even in the air, even with their fingers: trains,
three-cornered sails, trumpets, cymbals, the whole orchestra.
They say: you draw, you.

If you were born and lived somewhere else
you might not understand the fear of courage.

Hygiene

Today for the first time in months it stopped at one pack.
This is how it sounds best, when the impersonal form
gets into the ear by itself, when it speaks by itself.
Until recently the word "we" wasn't so annoying,
but just listen to something like this:
today we have smoked only twenty.
Quite as if the author had asked for the floor
in order to announce the projected estimates of consumption
    in the current year,
whereas he wants to speak unasked.
So hang in there, my friend, hang in there,
smoke, but not much; speak, but unobtrusively!

Potatoes

My son won't write a poem about a coconut.
I'm running out of words myself.
Still, if he wanted to paint a picture
with the texture of a ripe orange,
then by all means: just let him get hold of a golden lemon,
and in a moment a warm wind
the color of the setting sun will clothe it in a dress.
Imagination, mother of our life,
blow us more and more improbable landscapes!

In the Provinces

The Municipal Cooperative For Housing Economy at Otwock
GREETS THE BROTHERLY NATIONS OF THE SOCIALIST COUNTRIES
with each of the forty-eight letters fixed on a separate pole,
only the spaces between the words have no posts.
It's May 11, 1979.
The poles stuck in the lawn form a breakwater.
The Municipal Cooperative has been greeting the brotherly
    nations for more than three weeks,
but they still don't know anything about it.

One Day

One day I'll open the world
and step inside as if coming home,
and I won't be ashamed
of my mouth's voice and my heart's,
of any word;

I'll ask the world for an account —
a report on the time
I wasn't there,
I'll say: "World, tell me
what was, when I was not?"

and later still I'll say:
"Forgive me, world,
up to now I have been waiting
for the right train, for the whisper
of the locomotive of my heart,

and here I am, world,
perhaps a little changed,
devoid of irony
and maybe even more serious"

and there I'll end I suppose —
I'll feel weariness
in my bones, I'll see
affection in the world's face,
and I'll lack for words somewhat;

Communication Department

Leaves are lying on their backs, lacking the spirit of competition.
They live in unavoidable friendship,
they are friends in rot.
The international day

of the smell of leaves.
Memory in the air
and lots of Powązkis,
even across the ocean.

Postmen silently deliver
postcards connecting two closed circuits.
On such a day the high and the low
exchange juices and thoughts.

My mother would like to know the opinion of the maple nearby
on the question of the dissolubility of plastic,
decomposition of dentures and
how well grounded

is democracy anyway?
She doesn't have to get the reply instantly,
she can get the reply later.
The bottom line is that

the transmission goes on. Transfusion?
Transit. Bah, perhaps all love
is born
because of this trance

without end. You see it now?
You're grounded.
But don't worry, you too
are its multicolored conduit!

Confirmation

for E. and M.

I got boozed up because of Stasio.
He was just a few hours old, and after a week
he was a week old, and squawked a bit
at home when he woke up,
before he was fed.

Why make things prettier
than they are? Starting with birth
when doctors and nurses
press on the helpless belly —
press, what other way is there —
until death, with itinerant cancer
slowly taking over
the body, the skin
changing color in just seconds.
Until the latest possible death?

The past tense turns imperceptibly
into the present
continuous, as if it all were happening
in language: I have seen —
yesterday I saw —
forever means: I know.
Forever — that is, for good?

Little head observed
through the crack in Marek's door,
who moved his work to the kitchen —
why make even prettier
what has already turned out pretty well?

Someone from elsewhere
turns into a voiceless whisper,
while you're just pupating into words,
even if the day after tomorrow
they'll only hiss and bite,

the stomach fills up, the body,
in turn or simultaneously
remembers and betrays
more than you'd expect, cries,
wakes recklessly, and drifts into sleep.

(1986–1999)

What We're Remembered By

First Sentence

Four years ago at Ustka
four of us were walking on the sand and
I began to write my second
story (the first had been
about an invented
and painful death, very short
and a failure). I said the
first sentence to Maciek:
"Three years we waited, before
our applications for permission
to leave the beach were examined."
He said it was a good start.
I don't remember what came later
or if there was any later, probably not.

I suppose I said it simply
because I thought it
impressive, regardless of what
our favorite type of
humor was (back then
a joke would devour anything).
What I'd like to know is
if it was real fiction, and if
Maciek really believed
I was up to writing it, and
if it was indeed impressive.

For why hasn't he ever
asked: "What about your story?"
And: "Have you got a second sentence yet?"
That might have encouraged me to work,
because I never liked to leave

people twisting in the wind.
And, please, consider conditions there
were excellent — everything
at hand: the beach, the wind,
paper for the application, and thousands
of people, like me, idly waiting
for someone's final decision.

This Is Certain

Young provincials have literary hopes.
They will follow their first lyrical impulses,
then they'll grow more bitter but thanks to that, mature.
Lyric poetry, they believe, leads to an understanding
of themselves and the world, to perfection.
They'll look suspiciously upon the avant-garde,
with some superiority, which will be reflected
in their modesty, their solid lyrical craft
and aspirations deliberately curtailed
(this much is certain: better a modest yet sound performance).

But they'll be full of enthusiasm.
And optimism.
Serious matters are at stake.
Far from the quarrels of the capital, they know what to think.
There are always landscapes on their doorstep:
woods, a river, puffy pancakes of cloud,
or even wooden fences nibbled at by time.

There are places, who knows,
where only what's good gets printed.
But that's a detail you can bypass and step into the field
through a hole in the fence, best of all on an autumn evening,
and look at the sky, or trees,
anything —
for everything reminds you of impermanence.

Two Poems for Suchy

The Desk

I only leave home on important business.
—J. smiles and says: "Aren't you funny!"
The next day, someone I know runs into me:
"They say you talked all night about democracy,
I thought you were more serious than that."
I still feel young.

Abroad, the world is different;
there you talk about humanness, think about
Polishness, and judge actions by their effectiveness.
"Over there, pal, you have your car, hop in, wife
and kid in the back seat, that's just how it is."

My friend has a desk to himself,
so he can really keep his distance,
and he never endorses anything;
because he makes himself a kind of desk within a desk.
And, "I can always quit," he says;
but J. sits quietly and doesn't smile at all. —

So for instance I left this morning to buy
some homogenized cheese for the kid.
I claimed my place in line and went out for the paper.
I open it and there inside
his little boy is coming ashore, saying:
"I like this Poland of yours."

Hello and Return

Andrzej's flying in the morning.
I never thought Chicago
could feel so close.
After all, the distance is enormous!
He says if I love him I'll come, even late.
Plane or no plane,
distances are the same.

So I take a taxi and go.
What is all this love
between friends, anyway, and how many
can one have in the end.
What bothers me most is the lights
at the intersections
aren't synchronized. One turns green
and the next is red, it's stop and go the whole time.
There are only a few places
one wants to go,
even on foot.

On the way the wind keeps pushing stronger.
These next two years I'll probably get
two or three letters, I'll stop being ashamed
to use this or that word.
If you love me, you'll come at ten,
is what it sounded like. I can smell gas

and through double windows I see, inside the bus,
a poster of a cat right by the driver.
In a few years I could be someone else.

A few more kilometers, the door, hellos,
and again I'll go out into the street.
I'll start a letter and forget it going home,
I'll shut the door and — please,
don't take another job like that again.

Old Frame Houses of Radość

"What's going on now?"
It was a question
addressed not to me
nor to my wife nor
to the child, who had been asleep
for about two hours,
though, asking it, Mother-in-law
turned her eyes on me.
It was a question to the world.

For a long time I'd said nothing,
but now the world
spoke through me.
It said: "It's me —
Jacek Olszanka, the husband of your daughter —
who took the lid off the stove,
and put my old shoe
inside." Whereupon
I left the kitchen
to grope my way
into the room with wife and child,
put the book aside
and once again rebuke you
with my profoundest
silence.

A Bit More Effort, Please

for K. F.

He could go to the Academy of Sciences now,
but says he's more relaxed
in Świerk: an hour
of work, then an hour
for himself—he can really
learn; besides, the computer is better.

During my month in London
I translated a few dozen poems
at the desk of the Gresham Hotel
in Bloomsbury Street where
I was a receptionist,
so I know the work he has in mind.

We shall all further our education,
go from the desk
to the toilet, with a book
and a pencil, mark and memorize,
and come back so the boss
won't notice, until we become
one of the best-educated
nations in Central Europe.

Between Bus Stop and Home

You go to visit your friend after a film screening,
your wife stayed at home alone,
your mother, you start thinking
when you've stepped off the bus, is in another town,
ill, yesterday you had a telegram from her;
between the stop on the 140a bus route
and your friend's home (passing, that is
a closed shop, buying cigarettes
in the kiosk before the building, even in the lift)
before you enter his flat and begin
the evening conversation with him and his wife, you're alone;
your child went to your wife's
parents yesterday, is alone,
without you and without his mother.
You think about all this before the door's opened,
as snow powders straight into your face, although
it is the fourth week of March, pacing out
this short distance between bus stop and home.
Suddenly you notice this everyday loneliness, contrary to
    your self, perhaps,
and contrary to those you're thinking about.

Domestic

A woman drags herself from bed.
You know, I think I ought to make myself some dinner.
But she doesn't have time
and dies between
two gestures: her mother's
and her child's, never discovering
who, or whose, she was
more.

Says the Son

She thinks I'm leaving, but it's
like blood escaping
through clenched fingers. Blood
of blood. This is how she sees it though,
even if I'm always facing her
and we catch sight of ourselves in each other.
But the true mirror
is me, so squeezed into the glass
that only a drop
trickling down is truer.
And I copy her light, and that
blood. I could reflect everything
this way, except a few words
for which she'll never forgive me.

Transportist

Does such a word exist?
That's right.
Such an awfully busy
fellow, rushes here
and there, can't even
see, forgets
that he really is
between, that is, nowhere.

He transports words (from mouth to mouth),
gestures (from mother and friends
to child), and his own child
(from home out of the city),
by public transport, in fact,
out to unpolluted air.

But all those things
want to stop somewhere,
they can't always be
the object of transportation;
words stay behind the doors
of strangers' mouths, gestures
get written in the air
by strange hands, and the child
asked at school
for his father's occupation
answers shyly "transportist."

Belated Letter

Oh Grandpa César,
why didn't you wait for me?
A single glance would have been enough
and today I'd know that I can, that I have the right to
recall your face, because I'd really have seen it.
Photos are old and dead,
and Mother's stories rarer and rarer.
A single sentence would have been enough,
would have been repeated to me, for sure.

You know, Uncle Marcel — when I was there
for the first time — drew me the whole family tree
(I wanted to draw him one too,
but was ashamed: Mama, Grandma —
he already had Grandma anyway, since she was your wife —
Father, and Chaim and Fajga, his parents,
of whom, as about him, I know nothing to this day
— and that was everybody), and I looked and looked
surprised to find myself on this
big piece of paper, just below Mama,
and that in one family
there could be so many people.

You were of course much higher and deeper.
Everyone spoke of you
with respect and love, and I felt
that you had an artistic soul,
and I was proud.

I think that in a decent French family
in those days too, to marry
a Jewess wasn't easy,
especially in a country

of which only the language was left
(although a friend says:
only the word *pan*, and front porches).
Mama was saying there had been two
wedding ceremonies — I suppose civil marriages
weren't so popular yet? —
ah, these compromises for the sake of the common good
and not irritating the relations, eh?
And when you came back from the war, supposedly
you told Grandma to scramble twenty eggs.
That always impressed me an awful lot.

I wonder why you
and not the other one, Father's father,
of whom I don't know a thing —
I don't know if it's possible to not know
so much about someone — except
that he lived, had a wife, a first and last name,
and that he had to do something.
So it would be even easier
to write about him, to him, than to you.
I could create myself, build myself from scratch.
And what emotions those would be!

Was Łódź such a grim city back then, too?
Of course I'd bring you here, to Otwock,
and show you, in detail, this place
where there's nothing to show, and would tell you.
Maybe this is where everything came from: there was nowhere
to go, nothing to see, one had to sit at home,
at most look out the window —

> fifty-, sixty-year-old frame houses, one or two floors
> of creaky stairs, exposed dumps and dead cats in the
> yards, and the ball that always gets away from the
> children into the garbage, some skinned pines, pud-

dles or dark dry stains after puddles, underwear on
the line. All this — through the window
and inside
the tiled stove, the bed, the square of cellar hatch on
the floor, and the bronzed strip of sunlight lying un-
der the wardrobe; dust.

My friends here know nothing about you,
or maybe I did once mention
the *Légion d'honneur*, the mustachioed lieutenant, Verdun and
   the Somme,
but at most once, and probably only to one or two,
I forget whom.
And even if they remember something of it,
they probably think I was boasting, who knows.
And maybe it really is making up one's own genealogy?

Later on, I was mostly ashamed
of not having learned your language.
Maybe Mama started to teach me too early,
when I preferred to grab a heel of bread
and go out to the yard (does it have to stay this way?
Colette once said I could speak
quite well). In the yard the children
reminded me too, calling
"piot-rhuzh, piot-rhuzh," as if they knew
and needed me to share their knowing
that you'd come from France. But soon
I realized it was a matter of another country,
that is, the other grandpa
(I don't know how come
they knew it so much better than I did).
But I don't want to blame Mother, I myself
have wasted many opportunities.

Oh Grandpa César,
why didn't you wait for me?
Your great-grandson hasn't even turned three,
and yet if I died now, I bet
he'd remember something of me.
So just a few more years of life
would have been enough, a totally new world
for you to have to learn again,
these ten years, let's say: the end of the war,
Stalin, and at home
a son-in-law who, I think, hadn't finished the fourth form
in *cheder*, a furrier, and finally me,
seven years after your death.
About Father's education Mother preferred
not to tell me, she was ashamed,
perhaps would have been more ashamed in front of you.
Grandma didn't like him, supposedly,
impossible for me to say, I don't know
if it's people themselves who bear all the blame
for unhappy marriages.
(I remember once he made me a *kogl-mogl*,
but would give it to me only if I said I liked him more than
    Mother;
I don't know if she remembers,
I remember that shame.)

It's May, a few days ago
the first heavy rains fell.
And even every drop has its prehistory
which allows it to assume its own shape.
You know, at times it seems to me I am
a cluster of gestures that convinced me,
of words, which by some miracle I remembered
and quickly clutched
so they wouldn't get away, and of a few silences
I haven't learned.

Why am I doing this, indeed, why?
In fact there is no me for you even more
than no you for me,
though at least I know that you were
and that you died.
Why am I writing this letter, this poem, this I don't know what,
which wants to open me up from several sides
at once. Maybe it should
just find itself a natural ending
and stop dawdling, hang you in a frame
of memories, on the wall,
as your presumed portrait
(along with those twenty scrambled eggs, let's say,
or some other wheedled anecdote),
but it doesn't want to, it wants to go on with the theme
a little longer, as if you really were
only a literary pretext, broad enough
to let us talk about everything.

You know, today I was passing by
Grandma, that is by you both
(forgive me, but I only just
realized that unless the graves
were confused, you're there together),
it was already dark, I'd taken a taxi
to get there before the child
whom I hadn't seen in a week, fell asleep.
I was riding by the wall
that divides the dead from the living
and I didn't know whether to believe
in afterlife or not.
Is it really our children
who carry us further along? Some trace
should be left imprinted,
though one may well ask — for what.
And what does it mean to be faithful to oneself?

I'm having a conversation lesson soon
and should think up a subject to talk about,
since it's June already and the students
want to get into university.
Did you enjoy those private lessons, the girls
coming to your home — now
Więckowski Street, I suppose, then what?
Did you have your real smile for them, and were the lessons
truly you?

What a coincidence that I do the same thing!
(Did you have to do it, too?)
Yes, I smile
so that it doesn't come out all wrong, and I collect, collect
all the pretexts for squeezing out words,
reasons for talking, for heavy moments of silence.
I remember writing a poem about this
that didn't come off. Lately —
but I'm in a bit of a rush now — I write
only when it ought to come off,
or when I don't know what will, out of curiosity.
But am I myself really me?

And look, I've thought about it so much,
and it ends by itself.

Great, Now What

You look great in this
green one, but your neck
still shows, and the
head's full of not quite
clear words (my head)
and it also makes the eyes
change color some
what (your eyes)

Other Half

Thank you, I managed to get a seat
on the right side, on the side of the river
which attracts the overflowing shoreline.
With the sign Riverdale and overgrown
rocks, the red-brick building.
With the sign Yonkers which turns
gently to the left, then disappears.
Thank you, I can watch. With the bridge
which we have laid from here
to the other shore, in the vicinity of Tarrytown,
with its almost imperceptible embankment.
And yet, the river sometimes appears
at the tracks, as a reminder,
and the steep hills on the other side,
unmoving, nod, the light alone
moved by their fate. And by
the river's? — take your eye off it
for a second — it gets away
at Croton-Harmon, under track three
at platform two.
                    If on the other side
I'd watch the houses, roads, the trees
stripped of their leaves, but shining
with this delayed December light, because
it's January now — here and there shadows
adhere to the trunks. On the rocks at Poughkeepsie
I could study the icicles because the sun
hadn't broken all the ice yet
and January is snowless. And the light,
bouncing off the water's surface, even
through the tinted windows, draws
my inattention. Because the river has
widened again and the power lines help it
not to lose the way. Thank you, I managed

once again to get a seat on the right side,
even though the far shore turns away and
floats out of sight somewhere to the left then
returns, straightforward, and the hills
stand just over the water soft strong,
not hills, cliffs.
But then on the river bottom, too,
things shift, the terrain changes,
the water's temper wavers. At Rhinecliff
the water's cooling down, as in that other Rhine, so
all the sun's for nothing. The water or the river? Am I
my body, am I my eye that's also
cooling but sees further off:
mountains and, right here, the ice flow?
And there's another bridge, frail, bright-dark
above the ice, with cars easing
into the air so clear and uncountable
that you don't know how to return
to a place full of individual days
and dreams that don't have time to take
like buds in April after a late freeze.
Thank you, today I sat on the right side,
on the side of the birds who don't feel the chill
and sit, feathered, on the water, paddle, flap,
look for food.

(1994, 2002)

From the American

Afterlife

A small cemetery in the area (South Hadley?), with quite a few — in fact, many — Polish names; the earliest graves from the 1920s. Were it not for the names, it would be hard to guess that all these people came from the Catholic part of Europe: where has all the richness and fantasy of the graveyards gone? Only the spaces the graves take up are bigger than in Europe, and the spaces between the graves, also bigger. The place looks austere and bare, spacious and empty, barely peopled.

Improper names

Transposing names and the way they sound — an improper thing to do perhaps? Even when they happen to belong to the category of so-called meaningful names? But the telephone directory, the Great Equalizer itself, the book revealing, if not quite visualizing, a bit of the system we all know best, wants this done its own way. There are eight Marhefkas in it, all spelled with an "h" and an "f". All eight must be descendants of peasants who, at the turn of the century, came here from Poland, a place where they still spell the word with a "ch" and a "w", according to the rules of Polish spelling. "Marchewka" means carrot. But this in English would have to be pronounced [maːˈtʃuːkə], in Polish a meaningless sound. In the family tradition, it has been clearly impossible to sacrifice sense and sound to spelling: all Marhefkas in the book, the way they sound and are pronounced in English, not the way they look on the page, still make sense, still mean carrots.

Forefathers, our representatives

A neighbor with a traceable Slavic name, this semester taking mainly math courses at UMass, half-French (the mother), half-Polish (the father), but born in America, where he is very likely to spend most of his life, going perhaps for holidays to France where he will feel French and where at his departure his French relatives will also treat him as their representative in America rather than an American. And he is likely to enjoy this doubleness, I suspect, even long after he stops being a math student.

Meeting people

Some ultimate criterion of translatability: "Had we met over there, would we be friends too?"

Among ourselves

A famous Polish writer I am being introduced to, in New York, just before a reading the three of us, Poles, are going to give there. He has been living in the States for nearly thirty years, but has not been read much, until recently, when he got that famous prize whose name people have generally heard. The other writer has been living in America for six years and has not yet received any prize that people in this country could have heard of. There are three of us, Poles, in the room, but the host of the reading series is American, so our small talk happens in the lingua franca of today. The famous writer turns toward me and asks kindly in English: "Do you reside in Warsaw?" "Yes," I answer slowly, trying to gain time to understand what the problem could be — almost forty years away from Poland? a certain old-fashionedness of diction? a difficulty in visualizing those ugly cheap blocks of small flats most of us now live in, if we have been lucky enough to get them? my own inability to abstract from the somewhat different notion of "residing" and "residence" that for some reason sticks in my mind? — and then, still unable to decide, I quickly add: "But I like the verb you used." He laughs and — apparently feeling this is one of those misunderstandings that can be easily fixed — explains: "You live in Warsaw, so it is the place of your residence."

The zoo as text

One of the most amusingly innocent attitudes to translation — especially to poetry translations, perhaps — is trying to add explanatory words or phrases to what is being translated, an attempt to incorporate footnotes into the text of the original. This is frequently accompanied by the implied notion that nothing has really been violated. After all, is this not being done with good intentions? for the benefit of the reader? so that the reader could understand better? As, clearly, otherwise the reader would not have the slightest idea what to think. Therefore every spot of the text demanding on the part of the reader a little bit of effort, some more active reading, a bit of homework, is going to be leveled, or footnoted within. Why should you wear yourself out giving birth, honey, if you can get a caesarean?

Examples of such overtranslations can be found anywhere. I found one in a particular enumeration, before the cage of a Moustached Guenon, in the San Diego Zoo. It went, with the first three words capitalized, as follows: "Please do not: annoy, torment, pester, plague, molest, worry, badger, harry, harass, heckle, persecute, irk, bullyrag, vex, disquiet, grate, beset, bother, tease, nettle, tantalize, or ruffle the animals." Suddenly, all my ability to judge and distinguish between the so-called good and bad, the whole instinct of taste almost — was questioned. And I felt as if I were being grossly mistranslated to the animals.

A song

What shall we do with all our untranslated diacritical marks?

Untranslatability of squirrels

The gray ones in Amherst seem faded sometimes, as if they indeed once lost their more or less fiery-red color, the intensity of which may depend on the sun and season, the color so characteristic for the squirrels in Eastern Europe. In the old Łazienki Park in Warsaw there are plenty of them, and people try to feed them from their hands, unlike the way they feed the monstrously huge carp in the Park's royal pond, where people simply throw the food in. Supposedly the most effective way to make the squirrel come close, is to call out gently, several times, one time after another: "Basia-Basia-Basia," a more intimate version of the name Barbara. The name — or maybe the quality of its sound — is for some reason supposed to be more familiar to the squirrel than some less rustling Polish names. But the gray, kindly disposed Amherst squirrel of Amity Street, turns round and leaves us alone with our good intentions, unimpressed by our rhubarb literals: "Barbara-Barbara-Barbara."

List of poems, prose pieces, and translators

About the author

Piotr Sommer grew up in Otwock, a small town outside of Warsaw. He studied English at the University of Warsaw, and now edits *Literatura na Świecie* (World literature), a Polish magazine of international writing. He has taught poetry at Amherst College, Mount Holyoke College, Wesleyan University, and the Universities of Notre Dame, Indiana, and Nebraska-Lincoln, and has been awarded several prizes and fellowships, most recently by the International Writing Program at Iowa (2002) and the National Humanities Center, North Carolina (2004–2005).

Sommer's poetry collections include *Pamiątki po nas* (What we're remembered by, 1980), *Kolejny świat* (A subsequent world, 1983), *Czynnik liryczny i inne wiersze* (Lyric factor and other poems, 1988), and *Nowe stosunki wyrazów* (New relations of words, 1997). His poems have been translated into many languages, and his collections have appeared in English, German, and Slovenian. Other publications include books of literary essays, *Smak detalu* (A taste for detail, 1995) and *Po stykach* (Contact lines, 2005), as well as numerous translations of contemporary Anglo-American poetry.

Continued is **Halina Janod**'s first book of co-translations from the Polish into English.